MATERIAL WORLD

# MATERIALS

## at the
# BEACH

By
William Anthony

# BookLife
## PUBLISHING

©2019
**BookLife Publishing**
**King's Lynn**
**Norfolk PE30 4LS**
All rights reserved.
Printed in Malaysia.

A catalogue record for this book
is available from the British Library.

**ISBN:** 978-1-78637-447-9

**Written by:**
William Anthony

**Edited by:**
John Wood

**Designed by:**
Danielle Jones

## IMAGE CREDITS

Cover – LightField Studios. 1 & throughout – stuckmotion,1000
Words. 4 – Ivonne Wierink. 5 – DGLimages. 6 – Evgeniy
pavlovski. 7 – nayladen. 8 – wavebreakmedia. 9 – LDWYTN.
10 – GOLFX. 11 – STUDIO DREAM. 12 – Christin Lola.
13 – MsMaria. 14 – Bilibin Maksym. 15 – chaphot.
16 – Rawpixel.com. 17 – Peter Sobolev. 18 – WAYHOME studio.
19 – MSPT. 20 – Thomas Skjaeveland. 21 – villorejo.
22 – Praisaeng. 23 – Olga Danylenko, Sompoch Tangthai, Slay.

Images are courtesy of Shutterstock.com. With thanks
to Getty Images, Thinkstock Photo and iStockphoto.

# CONTENTS

Words that look like <u>this</u> can be found in the glossary on page 24.

# WE'RE LIVING IN A MATERIAL WORLD

Have you ever thought about what things are made of? Everything at the beach is made of something: wood, paper, plastic, glass... These things are called materials.

Everything at the beach is made of materials.

All materials have <u>properties</u>. We can describe a material, for example, how hard or soft it is, using its properties. Let's have a look at the materials at the beach.

Hard

Smooth

# A MATERIAL BEACH

Think about being at the beach. What materials do you think might be used for your wetsuit when you go swimming or surfing?

Surf's up!

Your wetsuit is made from a type of rubber called neoprene (say: nee-o-preen). Rubber can be a natural material that comes from rubber trees, or a man-made material. Neoprene is <u>man-made</u>.

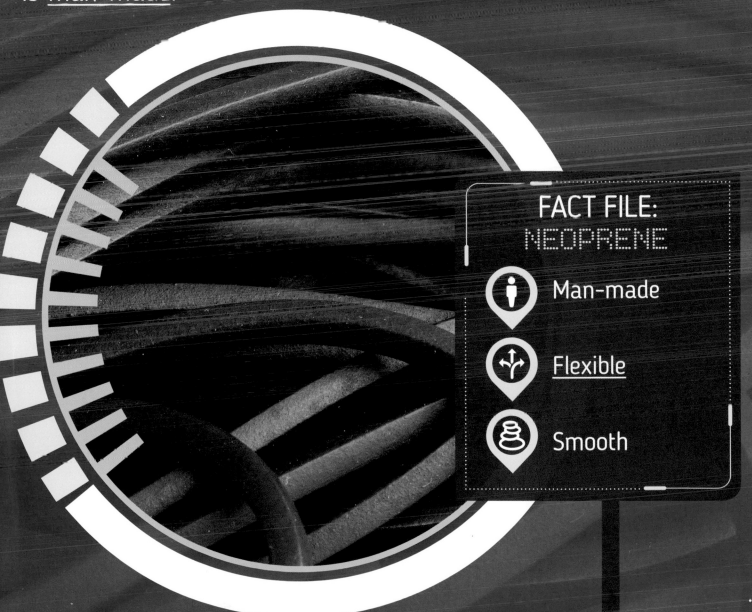

FACT FILE:
NEOPRENE

Man-made

<u>Flexible</u>

Smooth

# SUNGLASSES

It is important to stay <u>protected</u> when you are at the beach, especially from the sunlight. What materials do you think sunglasses are made from?

Never look directly at the Sun!

Sunglasses are normally made from plastic. Plastic is <u>rigid</u> and smooth, which means your sunglasses stay in the right shape and don't scratch your face!

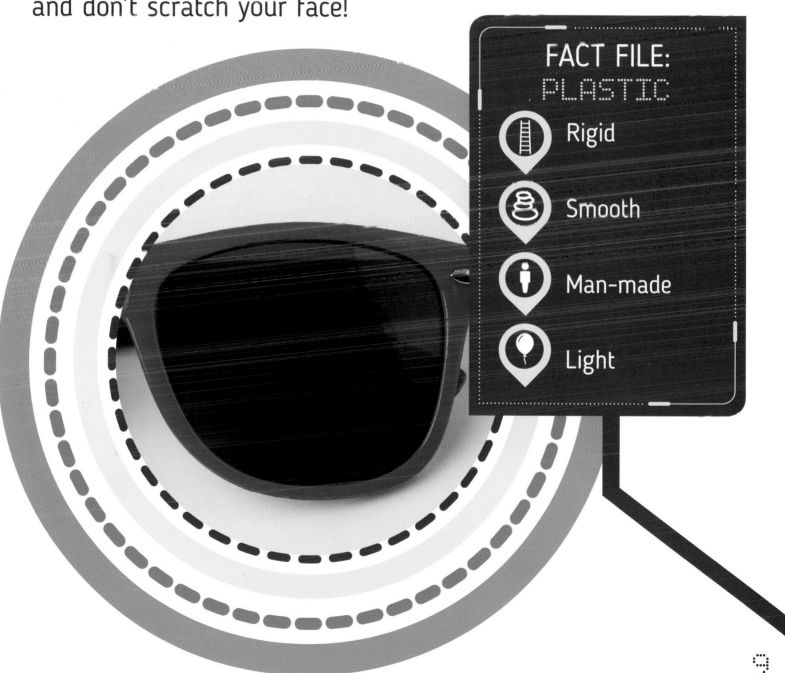

FACT FILE:
PLASTIC

Rigid

Smooth

Man-made

Light

A beach hat will also protect you from the sunlight. Some beach hats are made from cotton, while other beach hats are made from straw.

Straw

Straw is a natural material, which means it isn't made by humans. Straw is the dried stalks of plants.

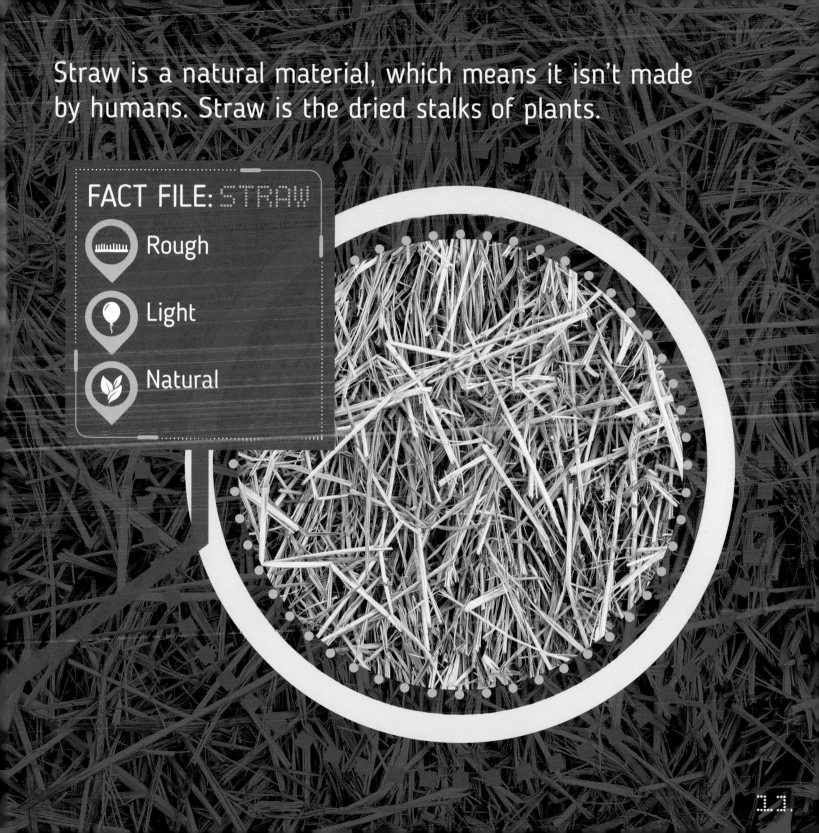

FACT FILE: STRAW

- Rough
- Light
- Natural

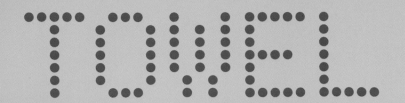

# TOWEL

What do you think your beach towel might be made from? It needs to be made of a material that can <u>absorb</u> all of the water on your skin!

Your beach towel is made from cotton, which is a type of <u>fibre</u> that has been <u>woven</u> to make a soft material.

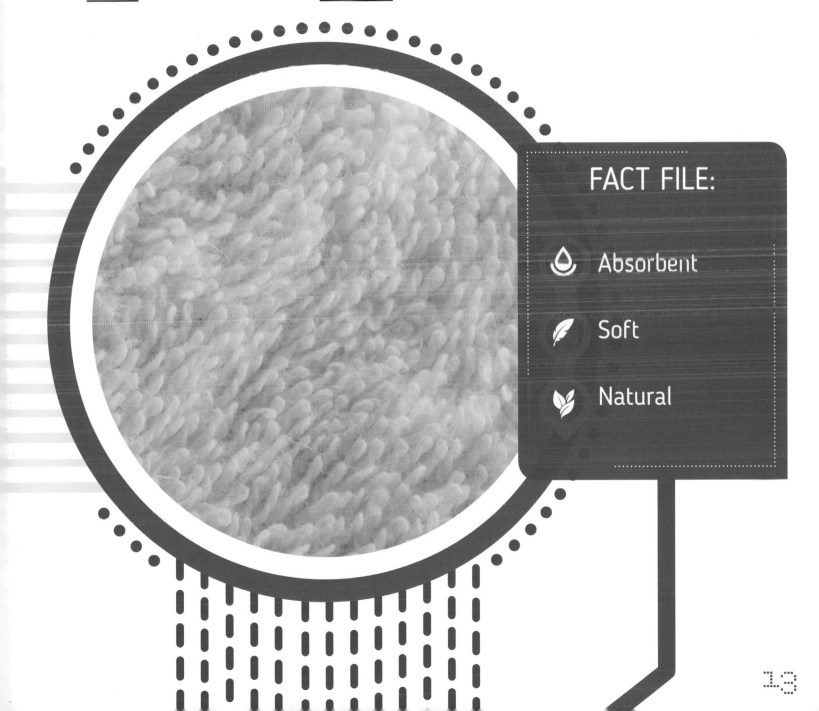

**FACT FILE:**

💧 Absorbent

🪶 Soft

🌿 Natural

13

# UMBRELLA

Sitting in the sunlight for a long time can get very hot, can't it? An umbrella can block out sunlight because it is made from an opaque (say: OH-pake) material.

Opaque materials stop light getting through.

Most umbrellas are made from nylon, which is a type of plastic. Most importantly, it doesn't let light through and it is waterproof!

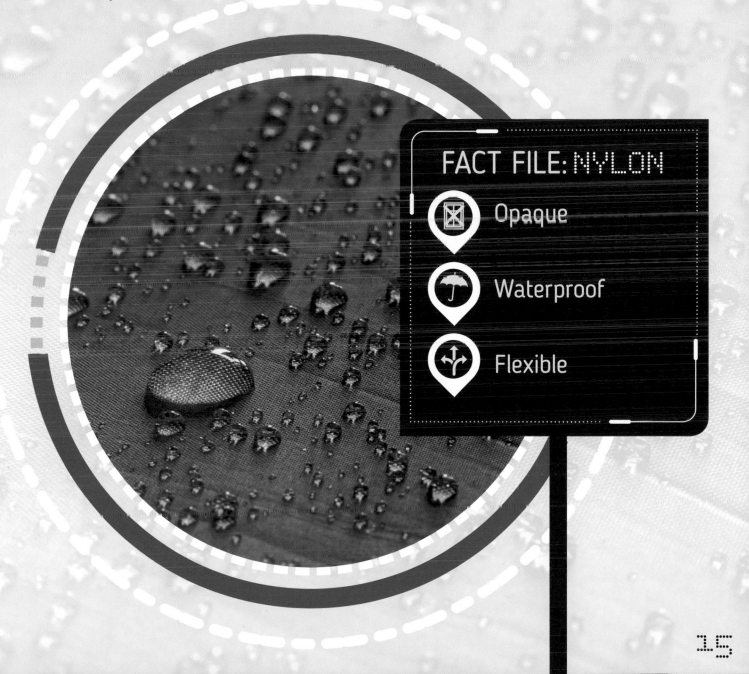

FACT FILE: NYLON

- Opaque
- Waterproof
- Flexible

# BEACH BALL

Why do you think your beach ball is bouncy and floats on water? It's because it is made from a material called vinyl (say: vine-ul).

Vinyl

Vinyl is very smooth and flexible when it is thin. When a beach ball is filled with air, the vinyl stretches and makes the ball bouncy!

FACT FILE: VINYL

 Smooth

 Flexible

 Waterproof

 Man-made

# ICE LOLLY

You can't go to the beach without getting an ice lolly; they're perfect on a summer's day! But do you know what the stick you hold is made from?

It's wood! Wood is strong and doesn't bend. You can also recycle it after you have finished. Recycling is when you use an old material to make something new.

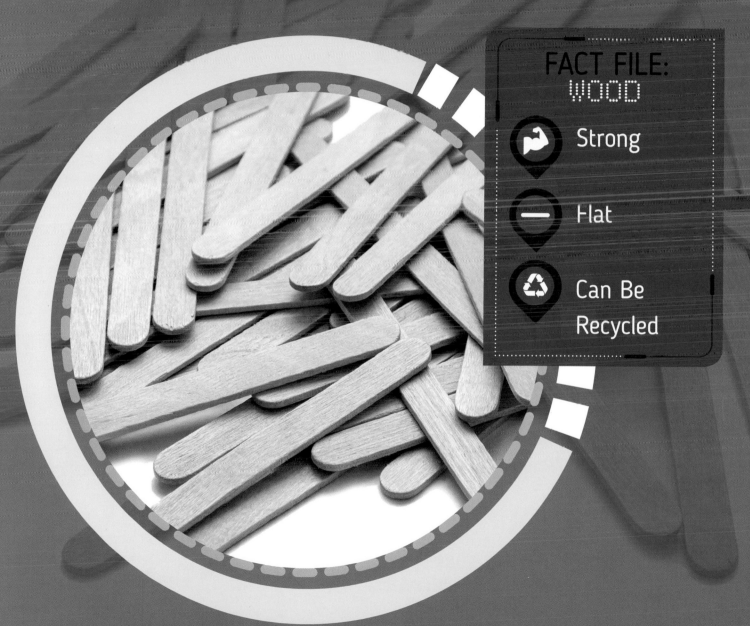

FACT FILE:
WOOD

Strong

Flat

Can Be Recycled

# BEACH WALL

Did you know that the sea moves in and out from the beach every day? This is called a tide. Beach walls stop the sea coming too far onto the land.

What properties would a beach wall need to stop water?

Most beach walls are made from mortar and either bricks or rocks. Mortar <u>binds</u> bricks and rocks together. These materials are hard and tough – perfect for standing up to the strong sea waves!

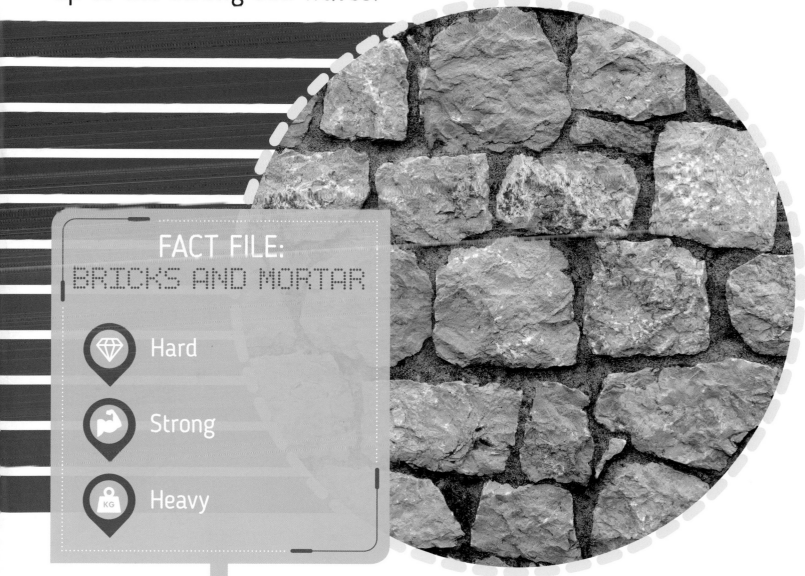

FACT FILE:
BRICKS AND MORTAR

Hard

Strong

Heavy

# MATERIAL MAGIC

Did you know that even sand can be used as a material? Sand is used to make glass! If you heat certain materials you can change their properties and use them to make other materials.

# ON YOUR BEACH TRIP

When you next go to the beach, see if you can find any materials that have some of the following properties.

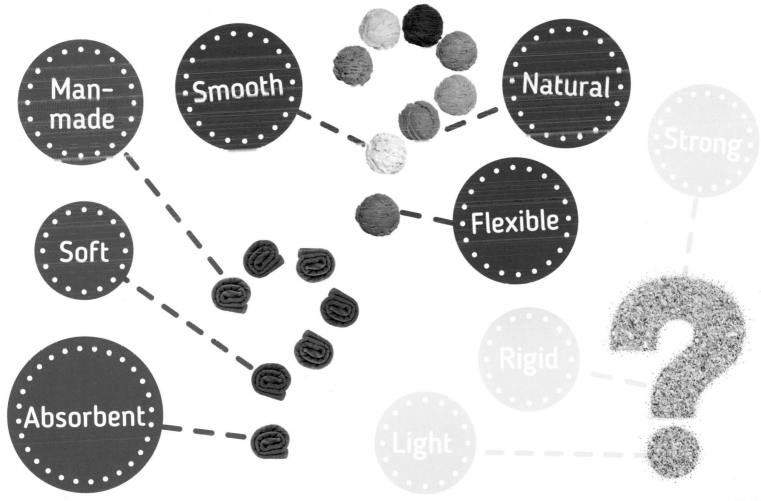

Man-made

Smooth

Natural

Strong

Soft

Flexible

Absorbent

Rigid

Light

?

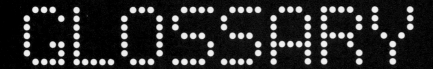

# GLOSSARY

| | |
|---|---|
| absorb | to take in or soak up |
| binds | holds together |
| fibre | things that are like threads |
| flexible | easily bends |
| man-made | not natural: made by humans |
| properties | ways of describing a material |
| protected | kept safe |
| rigid | not easily bent or reshaped |
| woven | made by passing threads over and under each other |

# INDEX